Tastes of
Anglo-Saxon England

Mary Savelli

Anglo-Saxon Books

Published by

Anglo-Saxon Books
Frithgarth, Thetford Forest Park
Hockwold-cum-Wilton
Norfolk, England

First Published 2002
Reprinted 2003

A Cataloguing-in-Publication record for this book is available from the British Library.

ISBN 1–898281–28-9

For Mother, who helped me with my cooking badge,
and for Stephanie, who gave me an idea.

Table of Contents

Author's Note

I would like to thank Terrie Holahan and Tony Linsell for their suggestions and comments on the manuscript. I would also like to thank my husband, Pat, for his encouragement, support and patience while I worked on this project.

Introduction

The Anglo-Saxon Kitchen

The nature of the Anglo-Saxon kitchen differed according to the social status of the household. For the poorest, it was merely the area surrounding the fire pit in a one-room house. Meals in these homes generally consisted of soups, stews, or porridges accompanied by breads and cheese spreads. Soups called for a single pot that could be suspended over the fire. Not only did this limit the equipment needed, but also it allowed members of the household to attend to other chores while the meal was left to cook all day. Bread and other baked dishes could be cooked in a Dutch oven or an inverted pot with coals banked around it.[1]

Wealthy families, including those of thanes, lived in larger more sophisticated buildings.[2] The thane's kitchen and bake-house were separate buildings, which reduced the risk of fire to the residence and also kept the home cooler in the summer. In the wealthiest households, a staff of servants prepared food. The cook, usually a man, could have several kitchen boys or scullions, who tended to basic tasks such as grinding herbs and turning the spit.[3]

Monasteries had kitchens similar to those on the largest estates. Generally, the cooking staff was comprised of monks working in one-week shifts. Their daily fare, like that of the secular population, consisted mostly of soup, bread and their accompaniments. Not only was soup easy for the *non-professional* cook to prepare, but a big pot could feed a large community with little difficulty.

Meals

Dinners in wealthier monasteries and in noble homes were served in two or more courses or *sendings*, with several dishes in each sending. The first course consisted of bread, served with soft cheese and other spreads, and meat, either stewed, baked in a pie or prepared as a pudding. Fish and vegetables would be served as the next course. The last course was a dessert, which included baked fruits and sweetened breads.

For a feast, meat would more likely be baked or roasted, and the number and variety of dishes would be increased. Like modern dinner parties and special banquets, Anglo-Saxon feasts were held for a variety of reasons, including victory celebrations, marriage feasts and holy day observances, such as Michaelmas and Easter. Trestle tables and benches would be set up in a large hall, usually heated by a central fire pit. The walls were decorated with tapestries and the seats covered with cushions. The tables were set with trenchers, stale coarse bread, which had been sliced to be used as a plate, and prized cups and goblets.[4]

Foods

The Anglo-Saxons left no cookbooks, yet it is easy to determine what they ate in general terms. Like most early cultures, grain or corn was the staple of life. The Anglo-Saxons had wheat, barley, oats and rye and used them to produce a variety of breads, brews (or pottage), and ale or beer. This was supplemented with legumes (peas and beans), roots (carrots, parsnips and turnips), *alliums* (garlic, leeks and onions), leafy vegetables (cabbage and lettuce), and dairy products (butter, cheese and eggs). The novice in Ælfric's *Colloquy* tells us that he eats meat, "vegetables and eggs, fish and cheese, butter and beans and all clean things".[5] This, with the animals named by the hunter and fisherman, gives us a long list of foods from which to choose.[6] We hear from the cook that most people knew how to "boil the things that are to be boiled and roast the things to be roasted."[7] And yet, we can find little detailed information on preparing meals.

Recipes

You may ask, if there are no recipes for food from the period, how can we recreate dishes that the Anglo-Saxons ate. While we cannot know for certain the original recipes, we can create some dishes with a careful study of the sources. Fortunately, Ann Hagen has already done a great deal of research in the area. In her two books, *A Handbook of Anglo-Saxon Food* and *A Second Handbook of Anglo-Saxon Food and Drink*, she provides extensive information on what type of foods the Anglo-Saxons ate. These books, along with the Anglo-Saxon medical texts that make up *Bald's Leechbooks* were my major sources of information. These texts provided information on what plants and other food sources were available to the Anglo-Saxons, as well as information on cooking methods.

Also among my sources are historical cookbooks and articles on medieval cooking. While most of these covered the 13th century and later, my sources included *The Roman Cookery of Apicius*, whose cookbook was used throughout the Middle Ages, and *On the Observance of Food*, a letter in which Anthimus discusses the eating habits of 9th century France.

From Hagen's books, I was able to form a list of the types of dishes I wanted to recreate. Modern cookbooks gave me a sense of proportions, cooking times, baking temperatures and the like. Sometimes these recipes gave me a rough draft for which I needed to document the ingredients. Sometimes, the medical texts yielded combinations that sounded like they would make tasty dishes. It should be noted that while I used the medical texts as sources, I am not trying to reproduce Anglo-Saxon medicines; I am trying to produce dishes an Anglo-Saxon thane would recognize and enjoy. My other goals were to create dishes an average cook could produce and a Modern diner would enjoy.

While I have tried to use only ingredients used by the Anglo-Saxons, some of the herbs mentioned in the medical recipes are now considered dangerous; others are difficult to find. For some of these, I substituted a spice with a similar taste; others are replaced with a food that fulfils the same function. For example, elecampane is substituted with anise to retain the flavour; plantain is often replaced with spinach, another leaf vegetable.

Measurements

Most of the herbs I used were dried. If you wish to substitute fresh herbs, a rough equivalent is ½ teaspoon of dried herbs equals 1 tablespoon of fresh. I used fresh onion, garlic, and parsley, so if you use dried versions of these, you will need to cut the amount. When a measurement follows the ingredient given, it is an approximate amount. For example, in the recipe for honey-glazed carrots, it reads "5 carrots, chopped (2½ cups)". This is because five medium carrots will be approximately 2½ cups when diced. If you dice five carrots and get 2¼ cups, it's close enough. If you use small carrots, you will need to use more to get the correct amount. British measurements (ounces and pints) and metric measurements (grams, millilitres, and litres) are also included for the major ingredients. The cup measurements are U.S. cups, which are 8 ounces, rather than the 10 ounces that a British cup holds. U.S. teaspoons and tablespoons are liquid (volume) measures, with a teaspoon equalling .16 fluid ounces or 5 millilitres, and a tablespoon equalling ½ fluid ounces or 15 millilitres. The serving sizes are also approximate. For example, my loaf of rye bread turned out to be roughly 9 inches across. If yours rises slightly less, it may be 8 inches or if it rises slightly more, 10 inches. Temperatures are given in Celsius (C), Fahrenheit (°F), and Gas Marks (GM).

Breads and Spreads

Breads (Hlafas)

Bread has been a food staple since the earliest times. The baker in Ælfric's *Colloquy* tells us that without his "skill, every table seems empty and without bread all food is turned to loathing."[8] All Anglo-Saxon meals started with bread. The four grains they used for bread making were wheat, rye, oats and barley. Wheat was the flour of choice, the fineness of which depended on how well off you were. In medicinal recipes and for ale, it is more common to see barley used. It was also used for animal feed. Barley, however, has very little gluten, a protein that helps bread rise. As bread, it was generally used by religious penitents and by the poor. It could also be used to stretch the valuable wheat flour. Barley flour can be found in specialty catalogues and baking shops. If you would like to try this type of bread, use the oat bread recipe substituting barley flour for rolled oats. Before baking, sprinkle with one teaspoon caraway seeds instead of rolled oats. All other ingredients and directions are the same as the oat loaf.

Bread baking has changed very little over the centuries. Anthimus tells us that "it is best to eat white bread . . . well leavened."[9] A recipe from a later period of English history states, "Take fair flour and the white of eggs and a little of the yolk. Then take warm yeast, and put all this together and beat them together with your hand until it is short and thick enough, and add enough sugar thereto, and then let rest awhile."[10] To leaven bread, yeast was used in both its dry state and in beer dregs. Other ingredients that helped the dough rise were eggs and salt. As with bakers today, Anglo-Saxons often sprinkled their loaves with seeds. This not only decorates them, but serves a practical purpose as well. Using a specific seed on a specific bread marks the loaf for identification.[11]

Baking was done in one of two ways. Large stone ovens were heated with the fire built inside them. Once the flames had died, the coals were swept out and the bread placed on the floor of the oven, baking as the oven cooled. Smaller households baked with clay or metal containers, which could be either buried in coals or placed near the flames. This last method is similar to modern gas stoves, where the oven compartment is over the flame. I bake my bread in a gas oven on a baking stone. Baking or pizza stones can be found in specialty catalogues and baking shops. They usually are made of a man-made substance similar to marble and evenly distribute the heat across the bottom of the loaf, creating a good crust. The crust would have a similar texture in bread baked on a stone floor or in a clay pot.[12]

Ætena Hlaf (Oat Bread)
(Makes one 9-inch loaf.)

7g (¼ oz; 2¼ teaspoons) dry active yeast
60ml (2 fl. oz; ¼ cup[13]) warm (40 to 46C;105° to 115°F) water
120ml (4 oz; ½ cup) milk
45g (1½ oz; ½ cup) rolled oats
1 teaspoon salt
3 tablespoons lard *or* other shortening
85g (3 oz; ¼ cup) liquid honey
1 large egg, beaten
120ml (4 fl. oz; ½ cup) water
170g (6 oz; 1½ cups) whole wheat flour
200g (7 oz; 1¾ cups) plain (all-purpose) flour, sifted
1 teaspoon rolled oats
2 tablespoons milk
1 loaf tin (8½ x 4½ x 2½ inch; 22 x 12 x 6cm)

Breads

1. Dissolve the yeast in 60ml (2 fl. oz; ¼ cup) warm water.

2. Set the milk in a pan directly over heat and heat until small bubbles form around the edge of the pan.

3. In a small bowl, pour the scalded milk over the 40g (1½ oz; ½ cup) oats. Set aside.

4. In a large bowl, combine the next five ingredients (salt, shortening, honey, egg and water) then thoroughly mix them into the oats and milk. Add the dissolved yeast and mix. Gradually stir in the flours. Stir until blended, 2 to 3 minutes.

5. Turn the dough onto a floured surface and knead until moderately stiff, 8 to 10 minutes.

6. Place dough in a large bowl that is lightly greased with butter; turn once. Cover the dough with a cloth towel and set the bowl in a warm place. Let the dough rise until it doubles in size, approximately 1 hour.

7. Punch down the centre of the dough and turn it onto a floured surface. Cover it with a cloth towel and let it rest in a warm spot for five minutes.

8. Shape the loaf and place it in a bread tin greased with butter (or shape the dough into a large ball, if baking directly on an oven stone. Sprinkle the stone lightly with flour before placing the loaf on it.) Brush the top of the loaf with the milk. Sprinkle it with rolled oats.

9. Cover the loaf with a cloth towel and set it in a warm place. Let the loaf rise until it doubles, approximately 45 minutes.

10. Heat the oven to 190°C (375°F; GM 5). Bake the loaf until it is golden, 35 to 40 minutes. If the loaf browns too quickly, cover it with foil after the first 20 minutes.

11. Remove the loaf from the oven when it is done. Invert the baking tin, sliding the loaf onto a wire cooling rack. Remove the tin. (If using a baking stone, simply set the loaf on the rack.) Let the loaf cool before serving.

Rigen Hlaf (Rye Bread)

(Makes one 9 inch loaf.)

7g (¼ oz; 2¼ teaspoons) dry active yeast

60ml (2 fl. oz; ¼ cup) warm (40 to 46C; 105° to 115°F) water

2 tablespoons liquid honey

1½ teaspoon salt

240ml (8 fl. oz; 1 cup) water

2 tablespoons lard *or* other shortening

85g (3 oz; ¾ cup) whole wheat flour

55g (2 oz; ½ cup) rye flour

225g (8 oz; 2 cups) plain (all-purpose) flour, sifted

½ teaspoon flax *or* poppy seeds

2 tablespoons milk

1 loaf tin (9x 5x 3 inch; 23 x 13 x 8cm)

1. Dissolve the yeast in 60ml (2 fl. oz; ¼ cup) warm water.
2. Thoroughly combine the honey, salt, shortening and the remaining 240ml (8 fl. oz; 1 cup) water. Add the yeast sponge; combine. Add the whole wheat and rye flours; mix well. Stir in the all-purpose flour. Turn the dough out on a lightly floured surface and knead it until smooth and elastic, about 6 to 8 minutes.
3. Place the dough in a bowl greased with butter, turning once to grease surface. Cover the dough with a cloth towel and let the dough rise in a warm place until it doubles in size, 50 to 60 minutes. Punch down the centre of the dough; turn it out on a lightly floured surface. Cover the dough with a cloth towel and let it rest in a warm place for 10 minutes.
4. Shape the dough into a loaf and place it in a loaf pan greased with butter (or shape it into a large ball if baking directly on an oven stone. Sprinkle the stone lightly with flour before placing the loaf on it.) Brush the top of the loaf with the milk. Sprinkle it with seeds.

5. Cover the loaf with a cloth towel and set it in a warm place. Let the loaf rise again until it doubles, about 30 minutes.

6. Heat the oven to 190°C (375°F; GM 5) and bake the loaf for 45 minutes or until it is done. If the bread browns too rapidly, cap the loaf loosely with foil after the first 25 minutes. Remove the loaf from the oven. Invert the baking tin, sliding the loaf onto a wire cooling rack. Remove the tin. (If using a baking stone, simply set the loaf on the rack.) Let it cool before serving.

Spreads (Syfligan)

Cyse Syfling (Cheese Spread)

(Makes 1½ cups.)

Bread was commonly served with butter, new cheese or some other spread.[14] When looking for ideas for a cheese spread, I came across a medical recipe calling for dry bread and cheese to be boiled in rose water.[15] If you are unable to find rose water, use a related flavouring that was available to the Anglo-Saxons, such as almonds. Almonds were suggested for upset stomachs, a property recognized in a 16th century treatise which recommended almond milk to "mollyfye the bely."[16]

225g (8 oz) small curd cottage cheese

225g (8 oz) cream cheese, softened

1 tablespoon white wine vinegar

1 teaspoon rose water *or* ½ teaspoon almond extract

½ teaspoon salt

¼ teaspoon ground black pepper

1. In a medium bowl, cream the cheeses until smooth. Then, add in the remaining ingredients (vinegar, rose water, salt and pepper) and mix well.

2. Cover the spread with a lid and chill it for at least one hour before serving it.

Hunig Butere (Honey-Butter)

(Makes 1 cup.)

Honey-butter was a popular spread throughout the Middle Ages. It is recommended boiled with sweet-flag as a cure for a cough.[17] I have used cinnamon, which was also known to the Anglo-Saxons, in place of the sweet-flag, as its flavour is similar to cinnamon.[18]

110g (4 oz; ½ cup) butter, softened

2 tablespoons liquid honey

½ teaspoon ground cinnamon

1. In a medium bowl, cream the butter until smooth. Add the honey and cinnamon; mix thoroughly until it is smooth.
2. Serve at room temperature.

Cipena Syfling (Onion Relish)

(Makes 1 cup.)

In the Middle Ages, onions and related plants were used more like a vegetable, as opposed to just a seasoning as in many modern recipes. While some may prefer this onion relish served with pork or beef, (or hot dogs), it may surprise you how well it tastes on bread.

1 medium onion (½ cup)

1 medium leek (½ cup)

1½ teaspoon prepared yellow mustard

80ml (2½ fl. oz; ⅓ cup) white wine vinegar

160ml (5¼ fl. oz; ⅔ cup) water

2 tablespoons liquid honey

1. Remove the outer layer from the onion and the leek; rinse the leek well. Chop the onion and leek coarsely.
2. Mix the onion, leek, and mustard in a medium non-metal bowl. Set it aside.
3. Mix the vinegar, water and honey in a small bowl. Pour this vinegar-honey mixture over the onion mixture.
4. Cover the bowl with a lid and refrigerate overnight. Pour any excess juice off of the relish before serving it.

Æppla Syfling (Apple Butter)

(Makes 1½ cups.)

While we are used to apple butter on bread, the Anglo-Saxons used fruit sauces on meat.[19] A recipe for stewed crabapples suggested this particular combination of spices.[20] Apicius also suggested combining these spices in a cumin-mint sauce to be served with oysters.[21]

2 medium cooking apples (e.g. Bramley or Spitzenburg *or* Winesap) peeled and finely chopped (2 cups)

240ml (8 fl. oz; 1 cup) cider *or* apple juice

2 tablespoons liquid honey

  teaspoon ground black pepper

¼ teaspoon dried mint leaves, crushed

¼ teaspoon ground cumin

1. Boil the apples in the cider (or juice) for 30 minutes or until they are soft; purée.
2. Thoroughly mix the remaining ingredients (honey and spices) into the apple purée.
3. Let the sauce cool first, if serving it with bread.

Peru Syfling (Pear Butter)

(Makes 1½ cups.)

This spread is similar to the Apple Butter, and goes well with roasted pork.

2 medium pears (e.g. Bartlett *or* Bosc) peeled and finely chopped (2 cups)
240ml (8 fl. oz; 1 cup) cider *or* apple juice
2 tablespoons liquid honey
   teaspoon ground black pepper
½ teaspoon ground cinnamon

1. Boil the pears in the cider (or juice) for 30 minutes or until they are soft; purée.
2. Mix the remaining ingredients (honey and spices) with the pear purée.
3. If serving the sauce with pork or another meat, serve it while it is still warm. If serving it with bread, let it cool before serving.

Soups and Sauces

Soups (Broð)

Pysena Briw (Pea Soup)

(Serves 4 to 6.)

Like many early cultures, the Anglo-Saxons ate one-pot meals, such as soup and porridge, as their daily fare. Even a poor household could afford a single pot to hang over the fire. Legumes, onions and root vegetables, which are easy to grow in a kitchen garden, and grain provide a nutritional base to which a little meat could be added. Wealthier kitchens would, of course, add more meat. One of the more common vegetable broths mentioned is pea broth.[22]

185g (6½ oz; 1 cup) split peas

Water, as needed

1 tablespoon general purpose vegetable oil

1 small onion, chopped (¼ cup)

1 carrot, diced (¾ cup)

420ml (14 fl. oz; 1¾ cup) chicken broth *or* stock

420ml (14 fl. oz; 1¾ cup) vegetable broth

450g (1 lb) ham, cubed

½ teaspoon salt

1 teaspoon ground black pepper

1. Place the peas in a large pot with three times the amount of water needed to cover them. Cover the pot with a lid and soak the peas overnight. Strain out the water and return the peas to the pot.

2. Cover the peas with water; bring them to a boil. Cover with a lid and simmer 2 to 3 minutes. Remove the pot from the heat; let the peas rest 1 hour.

3. Heat the oil in a small frying pan and sauté the onion.

4. Return the peas to the heat, and add the remaining ingredients (onion, carrot, stock, broth, ham, salt and pepper). Bring the soup to a boil. Cover with a lid and simmer for 1½ hours, stirring occasionally. Add more water to keep the peas covered, as needed.

5. Take out $^2/_3$ of the peas and purée. Return the puréed peas to the pot. Cover the pot with a lid and cook the soup for 15 minutes more.

Beanen Briw (Bean Soup)

(Serves 4 to 6.)

A similar recipe to that for pea soup is this one for beans, with lamb as its meat. The addition of ale was suggested in a recipe for boiled beans to treat tightness of the chest.[23]

185g (6½ oz; 1 cup) dried kidney *or* broad beans

Water, as needed

1 small onion, chopped (¼ cup)

1 clove garlic, minced

1 tablespoon general purpose vegetable oil

1 carrot, diced (¾ cup)

420ml (14 fl. oz; 1¾ cup) beef broth *or* stock

60ml (2 fl. oz; ¼ cup) ale[24]

225 g (½ lb) lamb shoulder *or* breast, minced

½ teaspoon salt

1 teaspoon ground black pepper

1. Place the beans in a large pot with three times the amount of water needed to cover them. Cover the pot with a lid and soak the beans overnight. Strain out the water and return the beans to the pot.

2. Cover the beans with water; bring them to a boil. Cover the beans with a lid; simmer 2 to 3 minutes. Remove the pot from the heat; let the beans rest 1 hour.

3. Heat the oil in a small frying pan and sauté the onion and garlic. Brown the lamb.

4. Return the beans to the heat; add the lamb with its pan drippings and the remaining ingredients (carrot, stock, ale, salt and pepper). Bring the soup to a boil. Cover the soup with a lid; simmer it for 1½ hours, stirring occasionally. Add enough water to keep the beans covered, as needed.

5. Take out ²/₃ of the beans and purée them. Return the beans to the pot. Cover the pot with a lid and cook the soup for 15 minutes more.

Hwerhwettan Broþ (Cucumber Soup)

(Serves 4 to 6.)

Another recipe using ale calls for cucumber, turnips and honey.[25] The Vegetable Marrow and cucumber were two summer squashes that grew in Anglo-Saxon England. While the following recipe calls for cucumber, you can substitute another summer squash, such as courgette (zucchini).

1 small onion, chopped (¼ cup)

1 tablespoon butter

770ml (28 fl. oz; 3½ cups) beef broth *or* stock

60ml (2 fl. oz; ¼ cup) dark beer (e.g. stout) *or* malt vinegar

1 tablespoon liquid honey

1 large turnip, diced (¾ cup)

1 large cucumber, chopped with skin on (2 cups)

1 teaspoon salt

¾ teaspoon ground black pepper

½ teaspoon anise seed

1. Sauté the onion in butter in a medium saucepan. Add the broth, ale and honey. Bring the soup to a boil.

2. Add the turnip; return the soup to boil. Cover the saucepan with a lid; reduce the heat. Simmer for 30 minutes; stir occasionally.

3. Add the cucumber and spices. Return the soup to a boil. Cover the pan with a lid and let the soup simmer for an additional 10 minutes. Serve while still hot.

Wyrtig Briw (Vegetable Soup)

(Serves 4 to 6.)

Anthimus tells us "barley soup is, as anyone knows who can make it, good both for healthy people and those suffering from fever."[26] This vegetable soup is based on a brew for lung disease, calling for sweet-flag, radish, carrot and barley meal.[27] Cress is added to take the place of one of the other leafy herbs in the original, lesser celedine, as it has a similar texture and was also used by the Anglo-Saxons.[28]

40g (1½ oz; ½ cup) barley

440ml (16 fl. oz, 2 cups) water

770ml (28 fl. oz; 3½ cups) vegetable broth

3 radishes, chopped (⅛ to ¼ cup)

2 tablespoons general purpose vegetable oil

3 carrots, diced (2 cups)

2 tablespoons cress, chopped

½ teaspoon salt

½ teaspoon ground black pepper

¼ teaspoon ground cinnamon

1. Soak the barley in 2 cups of water for four hours. Drain out the water and put the barley in a large saucepan. Add the broth and bring the soup to a boil. Cover the pan with a lid; simmer for 45 minutes.

2. Sauté the radishes in oil in a frying pan. Add the radishes, cress, carrots and seasoning to the barley.

3. Return the soup to a boil then reduce the heat. Cover the pan with a lid; let the soup simmer for 10 minutes or until the barley is tender.

Caules Broþ (Cabbage Soup)

(Makes 6 servings.)

This is a vegetable soup mentioned in the *Leechbooks*. Recommending that cabbage be boiled "together with young pig's flesh," the recipe shows that the relationship of pork and cabbage goes back to Anglo-Saxon times. [29]

1 medium leek, minced (½ cup)

2 tablespoons butter

770ml (28 fl. oz; 3½ cups) vegetable broth

110ml (4 fl. oz; ½ cup) white wine vinegar

1 (340g; ¾ lb) head cabbage, shredded

500g (1 lb) lean boneless pork loin *or* shoulder, cooked and minced

½ teaspoon salt

½ teaspoon ground black pepper

4 tablespoons (¼ cup) fresh parsley, chopped

1. Sauté the leek in butter in a large saucepan. Add the broth and vinegar and bring them to a boil.

2. Add the remaining ingredients (cabbage, pork, salt, pepper and parsley); return the soup to a boil. Cover the soup with a lid; reduce the heat. Let the soup simmer for 10 minutes, stir occasionally to ensure that the meat does not stick to the bottom of the pan.

Cicenes Briw (Chicken Soup)

(Serves 4.)

A common broth mentioned in the medical texts is chicken or hen's broth. The following recipe is based on one that called for "light meat", it's broth and the periwinkle, for which I substituted its better known cousin, the clam.

420ml (14 fl. oz; 1¾ cup) chicken broth *or* stock

420ml (14 fl. oz; 1¾ cup) vegetable broth

340g (¾ lb) boneless, skinless chicken breast, cooked and diced

60g (2 oz; ½ cup) dried breadcrumbs

185g (6½ oz; 1 cup) cooked clams, minced

150g (5 oz; 1 cup) fresh *or* frozen peas, cooked

1 teaspoon salt

½ teaspoon ground black pepper

1 clove garlic, minced

1 large egg, beaten

1. Place the stock, broth and spices in a saucepan and bring them to a near boil. Remove the pan from the heat; add the chicken and breadcrumbs.

2. Pour the beaten egg into the soup, stirring lightly. Add the clams and peas; return the pan to the heat and let the soup simmer for 5 more minutes.

Sauces (Seawas)

Wyrte Seaw (Herb Dressing)

(Makes 1 cup.)

Salads served with herbs, oil and vinegar go back to Roman times.[30] In keeping with the practices used in modern cookbooks, I have decided to list the salad dressings separately. You can serve them with the salads given in the next section, or serve them with any green salad. This first combination was suggested by a cure for a sore stomach.[31]

75ml (2½ fl. oz; ¹/₃ cup) white wine vinegar

160ml (5¼ fl. oz; ²/₃ cup) olive *or* salad oil

2 tablespoons cress, chopped

1½ teaspoons dried rosemary leaves

1½ teaspoons dried dill weed

½ teaspoon salt

¼ teaspoon ground black pepper

1. Thoroughly mix all the ingredients in a small bowl.
2. Cover the bowl with a lid and chill the dressing for at least one hour before serving.

Merces Sæda Seaw (Celery Seed Dressing)

(Makes 1 cup.)

This sweet dressing is based on a recipe that calls for parsley, celery seed and honey.[32]

90g (3 oz; ¼ cup) liquid honey

120ml (4 fl. oz; ½ cup) white wine vinegar

120ml (4 fl. oz; ½ cup) olive *or* salad oil

¼ teaspoon salt

1 teaspoon celery seed

1½ teaspoon onion, minced

1½ teaspoon fresh parsley, chopped

1. Thoroughly mix the ingredients in a small bowl.
2. Cover the bowl with a lid and chill the dressing at least one hour before serving it.

Hunig and Senep Seaw (Honey-Mustard Sauce)

(Makes 1 cup.)

This dressing, based on a recipe for an expectorant, can be used on salads or meats.[33]

60ml (2 fl. oz; ¼ cup) water

2 tablespoons liquid honey

120ml (4 fl. oz; ½ cup) prepared yellow mustard

½ teaspoon ground cinnamon

60ml (2 fl. oz; ¼ cup) white wine vinegar

   teaspoon ground black pepper

1. Thoroughly mix all of the ingredients in a small bowl.
2. Cover the bowl with a lid and chill the sauce at least one hour before serving.

Streawbergean Seaw (Strawberry Sauce)

(Makes 1 cup.)

The Anglo-Normans were known to have used a strawberry sauce with boiled beef, though this also goes nicely on a simple tossed salad.[34]

240g (8 oz; 2 cups) fresh *or* frozen (unsweetened) strawberries

240ml (8 fl. oz; 1 cup) water

60ml (2 fl. oz; ¼ cup) white wine vinegar

90g (3 oz; ¼ cup) liquid honey

½ teaspoon ground cumin

1. Place the strawberries and water in a medium saucepan and bring them to a boil; cook down the strawberries (about 20 minutes). Mash the berries; strain out the pulp and seeds, reserving the juice in a small bowl.

2. Add the honey to the berry juice; stir it to dissolve. Add the vinegar and cumin; thoroughly mix.

3. Cover the bowl with a lid and chill the sauce for at least one hour before serving.

Hindberige Seaw (Raspberry Sauce)

(Makes 1 cup.)

Raspberry vinaigrette was a popular salad dressing throughout the Middle Ages.

240g (8 oz; 2 cups) fresh *or* frozen (unsweetened) raspberries

240ml (8 fl. oz; 1 cup) water

60ml (2 fl. oz; ¼ cup) white wine vinegar

90g (3 oz; ¼ cup) liquid honey

½ teaspoon ground dried ginger

1. Place the raspberries and water in a medium saucepan and bring them to a boil; cook down the fruit (about 20 minutes). Mash the berries; strain out the pulp, reserving the juice in a bowl.

2. Add the honey to the berry juice; stir it to dissolve. Add the vinegar and ginger; thoroughly mix.

3. Cover the bowl with a lid and chill the sauce at least one hour before serving.

Salads and Side Dishes

Salads (Wyrtmettas)

Leahtrices Wyrtmete (Lettuce Salad)

(Serves 4 to 6.)

Lettuce has been used in salad since ancient times.[35] A recipe for an ointment that called for radish, cress, sorrel and plantain suggested this mixture.[36] I have substituted two more common plants for the last two ingredients, parsley and spinach.

½ head Butterhea*d or* loose-leaf lettuce, torn and rinsed (225g; ½ lb)

1 to 2 dozen spinach leaves, torn and rinsed

4 tablespoons (¼ cup) cress, chopped

4 tablespoons (¼ cup) fresh parsley, chopped

1. In a large bowl, toss the vegetables.

2. Serve them with one of the dressings found in the previous section.

Caules Wyrtmete (Cabbage Salad)

(Serves 4.)

Cabbage was often served raw with vinegar.[37] This cabbage salad was suggested by a diuretic made of "cabbage juice, some pea broth and vinegar and leek boiled with plantain and old cheese boiled in goat's milk."[38]

½ head of cabbage, shredded and rinsed (225g; ½ lb)

2 to 4 spinach leaves, torn and rinsed

1 small leek, chopped fine (¼ cup)

65g (2½ oz; ½ cup) fresh *or* frozen peas, cooked and cooled

55g (2 oz; ½ cup) feta cheese, cubed

60ml (2 fl. oz; ¼ cup) cider vinegar

120ml (4 fl. oz; ½ cup) olive *or* salad oil

¼ teaspoon salt

¼ teaspoon ground black pepper

1. Toss the vegetables.
2. In a small bowl, mix the salt, pepper, oil and vinegar. Pour this mixture onto the cabbage and toss the salad gently.
3. Add the cheese and toss the salad gently.

Hwerhwettan Wyrtmete (Cucumber Salad)

(Serves 4.)

Cucumber is another vegetable whose use in salads goes back to ancient times.[39] This salad was suggested by a recipe which called for a "green (unripe) gourd", mixed with wine and honey.[40]

1 large cucumbers, sliced (2 cups)

1 medium onion, sliced (½ cup)

½ teaspoon salt

¼ teaspoon ground black pepper

85g (3 oz; ¼ cup) liquid honey

60ml (2 fl. oz; ¼ cup) white wine vinegar

60ml (2 fl. oz; ¼ cup) water

1. Place the cucumber and onion in a medium bowl.

2. In a small bowl, mix the next five ingredients (salt, pepper, honey, vinegar, and water). Pour this mixture over the cucumber and onion.

3. Cover the bowl with a lid. Chill the salad at least one hour before serving.

Cicen and Wyrtmete (Chicken Salad)

(Serves 4.)

Chicken salad has been served since Roman times.[41] This salad was suggested by a recommended diet for someone with stomach troubles which calls for "vinegar and hard-boiled eggs . . . and herbs and lettuce . . . hen's flesh that is not overcooked and . . . peas and sweet apples."[42]

675g (1½ lb) boneless, skinless chicken breasts, cooked, and diced

1 medium Delicious *or* McIntosh apple, or other sweet variety, cubed (1 cup)

65g (2½ oz; ½ cup) fresh *or* frozen peas, cooked and cooled

4 hard boiled large eggs, chopped

½ teaspoon ground black pepper

½ teaspoon ground cumin

½ teaspoon ground coriander seed

½ teaspoon poppy seeds

¼ teaspoon ground mustard

¼ teaspoon ground dried ginger

¼ teaspoon ground cinnamon

dash of salt

¼ teaspoon liquid honey

3 tablespoons general purpose vegetable oil

1 tablespoon salad vinegar

4-8 full leaves of Butterhead *or* loose-leaf lettuce, rinsed

1. In a bowl, mix the seasonings with the honey, oil and vinegar. Combine this sauce with the chicken. Cover the bowl with a lid and chill the salad for at least four hours.

2. Before serving the salad, toss with the apple, peas and egg.

3. Serve the salad on a bed of fresh lettuce.

Side dishes (Gabote)

Hunigbære Moran (Honey-Glazed Carrots)

(Serves 4 to 6.)

The *Leechbooks* call for boiling various plants in butter and honey, a well-loved way to serve carrots. Anthimus tells us "carrots are good when boiled well."[43]

5 carrots, chopped (2½ cups)

½ teaspoon salt

2 to 4 medium radishes, sliced (^{1}/8 to ¼ cup)

55g (2 oz; ¼ cup) butter

85g (3 oz; ¼ cup) liquid honey

2 tablespoons cider vinegar

½ teaspoon ground cinnamon

¼ teaspoon dried mint leaves, crushed

1 tablespoon cress, chopped

1. Put the carrots and salt into a pot. Cover the carrots with water and bring to a boil.

2. Cover the pot with a lid; let the carrots simmer for 15 minutes. Drain out the water.

3. Sauté the radishes in butter in a large frying pan. Add the honey and vinegar. When this is blended, add the carrots, cinnamon, mint, and cress. Lower the heat and cover the pan with a lid. Heat the carrots through (approximately 5 minutes).

Gebuterode Betan (Buttered Beets)

(Serves 4.)

Another vegetable that Anthimus recommends is the beet.[44] This recipe was suggested by one, in which the beet's root is boiled with rue and pennyroyal in butter.[45] I have substituted rosemary and mint, two safer herbs with similar flavours.

2 beets, sliced (2 cups)

2 tablespoons butter

½ teaspoon dried rosemary leaves

¼ teaspoon dried mint leaves, crushed

1. Place the beets and herbs in a saucepan and cover with water. Bring to the boil; cook them until soft. Drain out the water and return the beets and herbs to the pan

2. Melt the butter in a small frying pan.

3. Pour the butter over the beets and toss the beets to coat them.

Ofenbacen Cyrfæt (Baked Summer Squash)

(Serves 4.)

This recipe is based on a dish for heart problems that called for cucumber, radish, turnip, garlic, and pepper boiled in honey.[46]

1 large cucumber *or* other summer squash, diced (2 cups)

1 turnip, diced (¾ cup)

2 tablespoons butter

1 clove garlic, minced

6 radishes, chopped (½ cup)

420ml (14 fl. oz; 1¾ cup) beef broth *or* stock

85g (3 oz; ¼ cup) liquid honey

¼ teaspoon dried thyme leaves

½ teaspoon salt

½ teaspoon ground black pepper

85g (3 oz; ¾ cup) dried breadcrumbs

1 baking dish (10 x 6 x 1½ inch; 25 x 15 x 4cm)

1. Preheat oven to 190°C (375°F; GM 5).
2. Spread 55g (2 oz; ½ cup) breadcrumbs in the bottom of a casserole dish greased with butter.
3. Spread the cucumber and turnip over the crumbs evenly.
4. Sauté the garlic and radishes in butter in a medium saucepan. Stir in the broth, honey, and seasoning. Carefully pour this mixture over the cucumber. Spread the remaining 30g (1 oz; ¼ cup) breadcrumbs on top of the cucumbers.
5. Bake the dish at 190°C (375°F; GM 5) for 35 minutes.

Beren Briw (Barley Pilaf)

(Serves 4 to 6.)

Barley is mentioned a great deal in the medical texts. A brew of barley and radish given for lung disease suggested this pilaf.[47]

85g (3 oz; 1 cup) barley

1 litre (1½ pints; 4 cups) water for soaking

4 radishes, minced (¼ cup)

2 tablespoons butter

60ml (2 fl. oz; ¼ cup) water

420ml (14 fl. oz; 1¾ cup) beef broth *or* stock

½ teaspoon salt

1/8 teaspoon ground cinnamon

1. Soak the barley in water for four hours. Drain the water and reserve the barley.

2. Melt the butter in a medium saucepan; sauté the radish.

3. Stir in the remaining ingredients (barley, water, stock, salt and cinnamon). Bring the mixture to a boil.

4. Reduce the heat. Cover the pan with a lid and let the mixture simmer 40 to 60 minutes, or until the barley is tender.

Swamma Hlaf (Mushroom Dressing)

(Makes 2½ cups.)

This dressing was suggested by a poultice made of bread, mushrooms and salt.[48] It can be served with pork or used as a stuffing for chicken.

1 small onion, chopped (¼ cup)

65g (2½ oz; 1 cup) mushrooms, diced

85g (3 oz; ¼ cup plus 2 tablespoons) butter

8 slices of whole wheat bread, cubed (5½ cups)

½ teaspoon salt

½ teaspoon dried sage leaves

¼ teaspoon dried thyme leaves

¼ teaspoon ground black pepper

1. Melt the butter in a large frying pan. Add the onions and mushrooms and sauté. Remove the pan from the heat.
2. Stir the bread cubes into the onions and mushrooms.
3. Toss the bread cubes and mushrooms with the seasonings.

Main Courses

Fish (Fisc)

Leaxes Hlaf (Salmon Cakes)

(Makes 6 to 8 patties.)

We know the Anglo-Saxons served seafood in some sort of loaf from the term *osterhlaf.*[49] It is possible this was similar to a modern meatloaf or to the fish dumplings made by Apicius with flaked fish, flour and spices.[50] I have chosen to make loaves from salmon and oatmeal, shaping them as individual patties or cakes, which are browned and cooked in a frying pan.[51] Salmon is a seafood mentioned by Ælfric, as well as the *Leechbooks.*[52]

400g (14 oz) salmon

1 large egg, beaten

1 tablespoon onion, minced

20 to 40g (¾ to 1½ oz; ¼ to ½ cup) oatmeal

1 to 2 tablespoons general purpose vegetable oil

1. Preheat oven to 180C (350°; GM4). Place the salmon in a small greased ovenproof dish and bake until internal temperature reaches 65C-80C (150°-175°F), approximately 30 minutes. Break the salmon into small flakes with a fork.

2. In a large bowl, mix the salmon with the egg and onion. Add enough oatmeal to create a firm texture. Form into patties approximately 7cm / 3 inches across.

3. Heat the oil in a large frying pan; brown the patties on both sides. Cover the pan with a lid; lower the heat. Cook the patties in the covered pan until they are heated through, approximately 15 minutes.

Ofenbacen Sceot (Baked Trout)

(Serves 4.)

Milk-based casseroles have been a way to prepare a simple, but tasty, one-pot meal since ancient times.[53] I have chosen to make a casserole with trout, one of the river-fish eaten by Anglo-Saxons.[54] Anthimus tells us that "trout and perch are more suitable than other fish." (see ref. page 65) The seasonings used here are based on a brew that calls for thyme, milk and wheat meal.[55]

450g (1 lb) trout fillet *or* other white fish

1 tablespoon butter

220ml (8 fl. oz; 1 cup) milk

2 tablespoons plain (all-purpose) flour

¼ teaspoon salt

1 clove garlic, minced

¼ teaspoon ground black pepper

¼ teaspoon dried thyme leaves

4 tablespoons (¼ cup) green onions, chopped

1 baking dish (10 x 6 x 1½ inch; 25 x 15 x 4cm)

1. Preheat oven to 180°C (350°F; GM 4).

2. Place the fish in a baking dish. Dot the upper side of the fish with butter.

3. In a saucepan, stir a little milk into the flour to make a smooth paste; then stir in the remaining milk. Cook the mixture over a medium heat, stirring constantly until it thickens and bubbles. Cook the mixture one minute longer and remove from heat.

4. Stir the seasonings into the milk-flour mixture and pour it over the fish. Bake the fish at 180°C (350°F; GM 4) for 30 to 35 minutes.

Roasts (Flæscmettas)

Bræde Cicen (Roasted Chicken)

(Serves 4.)

Roasted meat had a special status, as stewed meat was the normal faire.[56] Anthimus tells us that chickens are especially good roasted.[57] A medical recipe calling for chicken meat ground with honey, bayberries and mastic suggested the seasoning for this chicken dish.[58] I have substituted the more common spices, clove and cinnamon, which were available to the Anglo-Saxons and have similar flavours to those named in the original recipe.[59]

1 chicken (broiler-fryer) 1 kg (2½ lbs.)

120ml (4 fl. oz; ½ cup) general purpose vegetable oil

60ml (2 fl. oz; ¼ cup) cider vinegar

2 tablespoons liquid honey

½ teaspoon ground cloves

1 teaspoon ground cinnamon

1. Preheat oven to 190°C (375°F; GM 5).
2. Place the chicken, breast side up, on a rack in a shallow roasting pan.
3. Mix the remaining ingredients (oil, vinegar, honey and spices); brush the mixture onto the chicken.
4. Roast the chicken uncovered at 190°C (375°F; 5 GM) for 1½ hours, or until juices run clear, basting it with its drippings several times.
5. Let the chicken stand for 10 minutes before serving.

Bræde Eofor (Pork Roast)

(Serves 4.)

Pork was a favorite meat to roast for feasts and Anthimus tells us that the "loin of pork is best eaten roasted."[60] Marinades containing salt, vinegar and herbs were used to enhance the flavours of the meat.[61] This marinade is based on a list of easily digested foods including clear wine, cress, honey and sweet apples.[62]

½ teaspoon salt

60ml (2 fl. oz; ¼ cup) general purpose vegetable oil

1 tablespoon liquid honey

60ml (2 fl. oz; ¼ cup) white wine vinegar

180ml (6 fl. oz; ¾ cup) dry white wine *or* white grape juice

½ teaspoon ground cinnamon

¼ teaspoon ground black pepper

¼ teaspoon dried rosemary leaves

2 tablespoons cress, chopped

1 small cooking apple (e.g. Bramley or Spitzenburg *or* Winesap) chopped (½ to ¾ cup)

1 kg (2 lbs.) lean boneless pork loin *or* shoulder

1. Place the roast in a large container.
2. Mix the remaining ingredients (oil, honey, wine, apple and seasonings); pour the marinade over the roast. Cover the container with a lid. Place the roast in the refrigerate and marinade for at least four hours.
3. Put the roast in a roasting pan and cover with a lid or aluminium foil. Bake in a preheated oven, 160°C (325°F; GM 3), for 1 to 1½ hours or until the centre temperature has reach 75°C (170°F).
4. Let the roast stand for 10 minutes before serving.

Bræde Sceapen Flæsc (Lamb Roast)

(Serves 4 to 6.)

Another roasted meat recommended by Anthimus is lamb.[63] This recipe was suggested by a drink for jaundice made of coriander, sage, honey and *beor* and served with "sheep's flesh".[64] I decided to use cider for *beor*, following Hagen's translation of the word.[65]

1½ to 2 kg (3 to 4 lbs.) lamb shoulder *or* loin

2 tablespoons general purpose vegetable oil

1 medium onion, chopped (½ cup)

420ml (14 fl. oz; 1¾ cup) beef broth *or* stock

¼ teaspoon ground coriander seed

¼ teaspoon dried sage leaves

3 tablespoons plain (all-purpose) flour

1½ teaspoon salt

¼ teaspoon ground black pepper

240ml (8 fl. oz; 1 cup) cider *or* apple juice

4 carrots, chopped (2 cups)

1. Preheat oven to 180°C (350°F; GM 4).
2. Place the meat in a roasting pan.
3. Thoroughly mix the remaining ingredients (oil, onion, stock, flour, cider, carrots and seasonings). Pour this mixture over the meat.
4. Cover the meat with a lid or aluminium foil; bake in a 180°C (350°F; GM 4) oven for three hours or until the centre temperature is 70 to 75°C(160 to 165°F) for rare or 80°C (175 to 180°F) for well done.
5. Let the roast stand for 10 minutes before serving.

Delicacies (Smeamettas)

Cyse Briw (Cheese Custard)

(Serves 4 to 6.)

Egg custards have been served as entrées since Roman times.[66] A recipe calling for boiling cheese and forming "little cakes" suggested this cheese custard.[67]

450g (1 lb) mild white *or* yellow cheddar cheese, cubed

225g (8 oz) cottage cheese

85g (3 oz) cream cheese, cubed

6 large eggs

55g (2 oz; ½ cup) plain (all-purpose) flour, sifted

¼ teaspoon salt

¼ teaspoon ground black pepper

⅛ teaspoon celery seed

⅛ teaspoon ground cumin

⅛ teaspoon ground mustard

1 clove garlic, minced

1½ tablespoon onion, minced

1 tablespoon dry breadcrumbs

2 tablespoons butter

1 baking dish (10 x 6 x 1½ inch; 25 x 15 x 4cm)

1. Preheat oven to 180°C (350°F; GM 4).
2. Put the cheeses in a well-buttered casserole dish.
3. In a medium bowl, mix the eggs and seasonings well. Pour this mixture over the cheeses.
4. Top the cheeses with pats of butter and sprinkle the top with breadcrumbs. Bake the custard uncovered for about one hour in 180°C (350°F; GM 4) oven. Let it stand for five minutes before serving.

Cicen mid Đicce Broð (Chicken and Gravy)

(Serves 4.)

Another ancient dish is poultry served with gravy, a thickened sauce made with drippings.[68] This chicken dish was brought to mind by chickens that were stewed in milk and a brew calling for meal, salt and cream, boiled lightly until it thickened.[69]

2 boneless and skinless chicken breasts, halved (675g; 1½ lbs)

55g (2 oz; ¼ cup) butter

4 radishes, chopped fine (¼ cup)

2 cloves of garlic, minced

30g (1 oz; ¼ cup) plain (all-purpose) flour

½ ltr (16 fl. oz; 2 cups) milk

1 teaspoon salt

1 teaspoon ground black pepper

8 slices of whole wheat bread, lightly toasted, buttered

1. Bake the chicken in a baking dish covered with a lid or aluminium foil at 200°C (400°F; GM 6) for 40 minutes or until juices run clear. Remove the chicken, retaining its drippings. Dice the chicken and set aside.

2. Using stovetop heat, melt the butter with drippings in the baking dish; add and sauté the radish and garlic.

3. In a small bowl, stir a little milk into the flour to make a smooth paste then stir in the remaining milk. Pour the mixture slowly into the radish and butter. Add the salt and pepper. Stir the sauce constantly until it thickens.

4. Stir the chicken into the sauce and heat it through. Serve the gravy poured over toast.

Hierstte Cicen (Pan-fried Chicken)

(Serves 4.)

Apicius might have called this a *minutal* or rag-out; it's a dish of meat and vegetables, served with a sauce and something to sop up that sauce.[70] This recipe was suggested by a green salve which included chicken meat, asparagus, sage, cumin, marjoram, oil, celery, orache, and rue.[71] I have substituted the more common spinach and rosemary for the last two ingredients.

2 boneless and skinless chicken breasts, halved and diced (675g; 1½ lbs)

1 teaspoon plain (all-purpose) flour

1 teaspoon salt

1 teaspoon sugar

1 teaspoon malt vinegar

75ml (2½ fl. oz; ¼ cup plus 1 tablespoon) olive *or* general purpose vegetable oil

225g (8 oz) fresh *or* frozen asparagus spears, diced

1 stalk of celery, diced (½ cup)

2 tablespoons cold water

2 tablespoons plain (all-purpose) flour

120ml (4 fl. oz; ½ cup) chicken broth *or* stock

1½ teaspoon cider vinegar

1½ teaspoon liquid honey

¼ teaspoon ground black pepper

¹/₈ teaspoon dried sage leaves

¹/₈ teaspoon ground cumin

¹/₈ teaspoon dried rosemary leaves

¹/₈ teaspoon dried marjoram leaves

2-4 spinach leaves, torn and rinsed

4 pieces of whole wheat bread, lightly toasted

1. Place the chicken in a container and sprinkle it with the next four ingredients (flour, salt, sugar and vinegar). Cover the container with a lid and chill the chicken for at least 30 minutes, stirring after 15 minutes.

2. Sauté the chicken in a large frying pan with 45ml (1½ fl. oz; 3 tablespoons) oil, until the meat is white. Remove the chicken and set it aside.

3. Add the remaining 30ml (1 fl. oz; 2 tablespoons) oil to the frying pan and stir-fry the asparagus and celery for 1 minute.

4. Gradually stir the water to the flour so as to produce a smooth mixture. Add this to the frying pan, along with the chicken broth and seasonings. Stir the mixture until it begins to thicken. Add the chicken and heat it through.

5. Stir in the spinach; serve the gravy over toasted bread.

Saluian Ægru (Sage Eggs)

(Serves 4 to 6.)

This is the one recipe that needed little change from the original, medical recipe, which calls for beaten eggs fried in oil with ground pepper and herbs.[72]

45ml (15 oz; 3 tablespoons) olive oil

8 large eggs, beaten

120ml (4 fl. oz; ½ cup) light cream

½ teaspoon dried sage leaves

¼ teaspoon salt

¼ teaspoon ground black pepper

1. Heat the oil in a frying pan. Mix the remaining ingredients (egg, cream and seasonings) and pour into the pan.
2. Cook the egg, stirring to prevent it from sticking to the pan.

Mearh Smeamete (Sausage Casserole)

(Serves 6.)

Sausage is an ancient way to preserve meat and cooks have been making casseroles with those sausages since Roman times.[73] The Anglo-Normans continued this practice, baking dishes of ground pork and spices.[74]

1 small onion, chopped (¼ cup)

1 tablespoon general purpose vegetable oil

450g (1 lb) pork sausage (USA - soft *or* country) cut up

1 large cooking apple (e.g. Bramley / Spitzenburg / Winesap) chopped (1¼ to 1½ cups)

Delicacies

½ teaspoon salt

¼ teaspoon ground black pepper

½ teaspoon ground cinnamon

¼ teaspoon ground cardamom

2 tablespoons white wine vinegar

55g (2 oz; ¼ cup) butter

30g (1 oz; ¼ cup) plain (all-purpose) flour

½ ltr (16 oz; 2 cups) milk

4 to 5 slices bread, cubed (2 cups)

1 baking dish (10 x 6 x 1½ inch; 25 x 15 x 4cm)

1. Preheat oven to 190°C (375°F; GM 5).

2. Grease a casserole dish with butter and line the bottom of the dish with half (1 cup) of the bread.

3. Heat the oil in a large frying pan and sauté the onion. Brown the sausage. Remove the pan from the heat.

4. Stir the apple into the sausage and spoon this mixture into the casserole dish.

5. Sprinkle the sausage-apple mix with the seasonings and vinegar; set the dish aside.

6. In a saucepan, melt the butter, stirring in the flour. Add the milk all at once. Stir the milk until bubbly; then spoon this mixture onto the sausage and apple.

7. Top the casserole with the remaining half (1 cup) of the bread and bake it uncovered at 190°C (375°F; GM 5) for 30 minutes.

Hriðer Smeamete (Beef Casserole)

(Serves 4 to 6.)

The Anglo-Saxons had a taste for fruit cooked with their meat.[75] This beef and fruit casserole was suggested by a poultice made of oil, wine, butter, grapes and saffron.[76] Anthimus recommends beef casseroles with similar ingredients, including vinegar, wine, honey and pepper.[77]

¼ teaspoon saffron threads

1 tablespoon hot water

1 tablespoon white wine vinegar

750g to 1kg (1½ to 2 lbs.) lean minced stewing beef *or* beef brisket

2 tablespoons general purpose vegetable oil

85g (3 oz; ¾ cup) dried breadcrumbs

1 small cooking apple (Bramley / Spitzenburg / Winesap) chopped (½ - ¾ cup)

35g (1¼ oz; ¼ cup) raisins

40g (1½ oz; ¼ cup) dates, coarsely chopped

85g (3 oz; ¼ cup) liquid honey

½ teaspoon salt

¼ teaspoon ground black pepper

¼ teaspoon ground cinnamon

60ml (2 fl. oz; ¼ cup) dry red wine *or* apple juice

2 tablespoons butter

1 baking dish (10 x 6 x 1½ inch; 25 x 15 x 4cm)

1. Preheat oven to 190°C (375°F; GM 5).

2. Crush the saffron in a small bowl and cover it with the hot water and vinegar; set it aside.

3. Brown the beef in oil; set it aside.

4. Grease a casserole dish with butter. Spread 55g (2 oz; ½ cup) breadcrumbs in the bottom of the dish.

5. Spread the beef, fruit, saffron-water and other spices evenly over the crumbs. Mix the honey with the wine and gently pour this mixture over the beef.

6. Spread the remaining 30g (1 oz; ¼ cup) breadcrumbs over the beef and dot the crumbs with butter.

7. Bake the casserole uncovered in a 190°C (375°F; GM 5) oven for 45 minutes or until done.

Desserts and Beverages

Desserts (Eft-mettas)

Bæcen Æpplas (Baked Apples)

(Makes 6.)

Some Anglo-Saxon physicians warned that raw fruit was bad for digestion, making cooked fruit more common.[78] If Anglo-Norman recipes are any indication, there were several of these dishes which included ample honey.

6 large cooking apples (e.g. Bramley / Spitzenburg / Winesap)

1 small pears (e.g. Barlett / Bosc) peeled and chopped (½ cup)

1 small peach, any variety, peeled and chopped (½ cup)

170g (6 oz; ½ cup) liquid honey

55g (2 oz; ½ cup) unseasoned breadcrumbs

1 teaspoon ground cinnamon

55g (2 oz; ¼ cup) butter, melted

1 baking dish (10 x 6 x 1½ inch; 25 x 15 x 4cm)

1. Preheat the oven to 190°C (375°F; GM 5). Wash, peel and core the apples. Slice ½ inch (1cm) from bottom of each of the apples so that they will sit flat in a roasting pan.

2. Combine the pear, peach, honey, breadcrumbs, cinnamon and butter. Stuff the apples with this mixture, generously mounding any remaining mixture on top of them.

3. Bake the apples covered with lid or aluminium foil at 190°C (375°F; GM 5) for approximately 30 to 40 minutes or until the filling is cooked and bubbly. Serve the apples while still warm.

Peru on Wine (Pears in Wine Sauce)

(Serves 4.)

A popular cooked fruit dish throughout the ages has been pears in a wine sauce.[79] This recipe was suggested by one calling for pear-bark, cinnamon, cummin, and pepper.[80]

4 small hard pears peeled and sliced – Conference/Bartlett/Bosc

60ml (2 fl. oz; ¼ cup) red wine

170g (6 oz; ½ cup) liquid honey

1 teaspoon ground cinnamon

½ teaspoon ground cloves

$^1/_8$ teaspoon ground cumin

$^1/_8$ teaspoon ground black pepper

1 baking dish (8 x 8 inch; 20 x 20°Cm)

1. Preheat oven to 180°C (350°F; GM 4).
2. Place the pears in a baking dish.
3. Mix the remaining ingredients (wine, honey and spices) and pour this mixture over the pears.
4. Cover the pears with a lid or foil; bake at 180°C (350°F; GM 4) for one hour or until tender. Serve the pears either hot or cold.

Hunigæpplas (Honey-Apples)

(Makes 9 servings.)

Honey-apple is the name of a sweet cake, a term which glossed the Latin term *pastellus*. I follow Hagen's suggestion that these cakes may have been a type of bread pudding.[81]

6 slices of whole wheat bread, diced

240ml (8 fl. oz; 1 cup) milk

120ml (4 fl. oz; ½ cup) cider *or* apple juice

¼ teaspoon salt

½ teaspoon ground cloves

½ teaspoon ground cinnamon

170g (6 oz; ½ cup) liquid honey

150g (5¼ oz; 1 cup) raisins

1 medium cooking apple (Bramley / Spitzenburg / Winesap) chopped (1 cup)

1 baking tin (8 x 8 inch; 20 x 20°Cm)

1 baking tin (10 x 10 inch; 25 x25cm)

1. Preheat oven to 200°C (400°F; GM 6).

2. Place the bread in a large bowl. Pour the milk and cider over the bread and let it soak. Cover and leave for 15 minutes.

3. In a medium bowl, mix the remaining ingredients (honey, fruit and spices); add this mixture to the bread.

4. Set the 8 inch pan in the larger pan. Carefully pour water into the outer (larger) pan until it is 1 inch (2· 5cm) deep. Place the bread mix into the smaller pan and bake both pans uncovered at 200°C (400°F; GM 6) for 45 minutes. Let the pudding cool for 10 minutes before serving.

Flete Estmete (Sour Cream Custard)

(Makes 1-9 inch pie.)

Sweet custards have been a favourite since Roman times.[82] This recipe was suggested by one calling for sour cream, honey and egg yolks.[83]

3 large eggs

675g (1½ lbs.; 3 cups) cottage cheese

240ml (8 fl. oz; 1 cup) sour cream

1 teaspoon almond extract

170g (6 oz; ½ cup) liquid honey

3 tablespoons fine dry breadcrumbs

2½ tablespoons sugar

2½ tablespoons butter, melted

¼ teaspoon ground cinnamon

225g (8 oz; 2 cups) fresh strawberries, sliced

1 pie tin (9 inch; 23cm)

1. Preheat oven to 180°C (350°F; GM 4).
2. Combine the cottage cheese, egg, sour cream, honey and almond extract; mix them until smooth.
3. Pour this batter into a buttered pie dish. Mix the remaining ingredients (breadcrumbs, sugar, butter and cinnamon) and sprinkle on top of the batter. Bake the custard uncovered at 180°C (350°F; GM 4) for one hour or until firm.
4. Cool and serve with sliced strawberries.

Gesufel Hlaf (Spice Loaf)

(Serves 6.)

Another type of cake was the Gesufel bread, a seasoned loaf made for feast days.[84] The spices for this sweet bread were suggested by a salve that included ginger, cinnamon and bayberries.[85] I have substituted cloves for the last ingredient, a safer seasoning with a similar flavour.

120ml (4 fl. oz; ½ cup) warm water (40 to 46C;105° to 115°F)

7g (¼ oz; 2¼ teaspoons) dry active yeast

55g (2 oz; ½ cup) plain (all-purpose) flour, sifted

55g (2 oz; ¼ cup) butter, softened

85g (3 oz; ¼ cup) liquid honey

1 large egg

½ teaspoon salt

1 teaspoon ground cinnamon

½ teaspoon ground dried ginger

½ teaspoon ground cloves

200g (7 oz; 1¾ cup) plain (all-purpose) flour, sifted

30g (1 oz; ¼ cup) walnuts, chopped

30g (1 oz; ¼ cup) hazelnuts, chopped

35g (1¼ oz; ¼ cup) raisins

40g (1½ oz; ¼ cup) dates, chopped

2 tablespoons melted butter

225g (8 oz; 1 cup) Devonshire *or* clotted cream

1 loaf tin (5 x 9 x 3 inch; 13 x 23 x 8cm)

1. Combine the water with the yeast in a small bowl; let it sit 5 minutes.

2. Add 55g (2 oz, ½ cup) flour to the yeast mixture and cover with a cloth towel; let it rise for 30 minutes.

3. In a large bowl beat 55g (2 oz; ¼ cup) of butter until it is soft. Add the honey, egg, salt, cinnamon, ginger, and cloves. Thoroughly mix the ingredients.

4. Add the yeast-flour mixture to the butter-honey mixture and combine. Gradually mix in the remaining 200g (7 oz; 1¾ cup) of flour and beat it for five minutes.

5. Add the nuts and fruit and mix them well.

6. Cover the bowl with a cloth towel and put it in a warm place. Let the dough rise for two hours.

7. Punch down the centre of the ball of dough; form a loaf. Place the loaf in a bread pan greased with butter; brush the top of the loaf with melted butter.

8. Cover the loaf with a cloth towel and let it rise in a warm place for 30 minutes.

9. Bake the bread uncovered at 180°C (350°F; GM 4) for approximately 30 minutes. Remove the bread from the tin and let it cool on a wire rack. Serve the bread with clotted cream.

Beverages (Drincas)

Medu (Mead)

(Makes approximately ½ gal.)

Mead was a standard beverage in the Anglo-Saxon feast-hall. This recipe is one I have used in my own kitchen for several years. While Hagen suggests that the Anglo-Saxons used bakers' yeast, I use it because it is convenient.[1] Baker's yeast gives a lower alcohol content than wine yeast, but the mead will still have a pleasant taste. If you wish to use wine yeast, use Mead or Champagne yeast.

While these recipes are suitable for a beginner, if you have no experience making wine or beer, you may find it useful to pick up an introductory book on the subject.

3 ltr (5 Imperial pts; ¾ gallon) water

1½ kg (3 lbs.) liquid honey

1 teaspoon cider vinegar

1 teaspoon rose hips *or* black tea

1 tablespoon hot water

1 teaspoon ground cinnamon

7g (¼ oz; 2¼ teaspoons) dry active yeast *or* 1 packet Wine yeast

5 litre / 1 gallon glass jug / demijohn bottle

1 airlock and stopper *or* 1 balloon

1. Make sure all the equipment is cleaned and sterilised.

2. Steep the rose hips *or* tea in 1-tablespoon hot water for 15 minutes. Strain out the hips / tea, reserving water.

3. Boil the honey and water in a large pot for 20 minutes (45 minutes, if using raw honey); skim off any foam that may form on top. Remove the pot from the heat and add the tea / rose hip-water, vinegar and cinnamon.

4. Let the liquid cool. Add the yeast. Place the mead in a clean 5 litre / 1 gallon glass jug / demijohn bottle and place the airlock or balloon over the jug's opening.

5. Once the mead has started to clear (in one or two weeks), siphon the mead into a new jug, being careful not to disturb any sediment. (You may need to rack [siphon] the Mead a second time, if there is a lot of sediment.) Bottle the mead in one to two months when it has stopped fermenting.

Moraδ (Mulberry Wine)

(Makes approximately ½ gal.)

This unusual wine was a favourite of the Anglo-Saxons. If you can't find mulberries, you can substitute another berry. I have made it with strawberries and raspberries, both of which were available to the Anglo-Saxons.[86]

3 ltr (5 Imperial pts; ¾ gallon) water

675g (1½ lbs.) mulberries

1 tablespoon sugar

225 g (½ lb) raisins

7g (¼ oz; 2¼ teaspoons) dry active yeast *or* 1 packet Wine yeast

675g (1½ lbs.) liquid honey

5 litre / 1 gallon glass jug / demijohn bottle

1 airlock and stopper *or* 1 balloon

1. Make sure all the equipment is cleaned and sterilised.
2. Crush the fruit in a large bowl and add half of the water (1· 5 ltr; 2½ Imperial pts; 6 cups). Sprinkle the sugar over the fruit; cover the bowl with a lid and let the fruit soak overnight.
3. Strain out the pulp twice, reserving the juice. Place the juice in a saucepan and bring it to a boil. Let the juice simmer for three minutes. Set the juice aside.
4. Boil the honey with the remaining 1· 5 ltr (2½ Imperial pts; 6 cups) water in a large pot for 20 minutes (45 minutes, if using raw honey); skim off any foam that forms. Remove the pot from the heat and add the mulberry juice. Cool the solution slightly. Put the raisins in a glass gallon jug / bottle and pour the liquid into it.
5. Let the wine cool completely. Add the yeast and put the airlock over the jug's opening.

6. After two weeks, pour the liquid into a clean jug, straining out the raisins.

7. After another week, rack (siphon) the wine into a clean jug, being careful not to disturb any sediment. (You may need to repeat this step a second time.) Bottle the *moraþ* in one to two months when it has stopped fermenting.

Wyrtdrenc (Bragot and Pigment)

(Makes approximately 2 pints.)

Bragot and pigment were flavoured ale and wine, bragot for ale and pigment for wine.[87] You may be familiar with Hippocras, or *ypocras*, one version of pigment popular to the present day.[88] This recipe is based on one for a drink for a wounded stomach and can be used with wine or ale.[89]

700ml (1¼ Imperial pt; 1½ US pt) dark beer (e.g. stout) *or* red wine

120ml (4 fl. oz; ½ cup) water

1 teaspoon dried rosemary leaves

1 tablespoon dried mint leaves, crushed

170g (6 oz; ½ cup) liquid honey or more if you prefer a sweeter wine.

1. Bring the beer or wine and water slowly to a boil. Stir in the herbs; add honey to taste. Let the liquid simmer for 20 minutes.
2. Strain out the spices. Serve the beverage either warm or cold.

Suggested Menus

Vegetable Soup

Beef Casserole   Rye Bread   Apple Butter   Honey-Butter

Mushroom Dressing   Chicken Salad

Sour Cream Custard

Bean Soup

Pork Roast   Oat Bread   Pear Butter   Onion Relish

Cabbage Salad   Salmon Cakes

Honey Apples

Cabbage Soup

Chicken and Gravy   Oat Bread   Onion Relish   Honey-Butter

Honey-Glazed Carrots   Baked Fillet

Pears in Wine Sauce

Cucumber Soup

Lamb Roast   Rye Bread   Apple Butter   Cheese Spread

Lettuce Salad with Celery Seed Dressing   Sage Eggs

Baked Apples

List of Ingredients

I have not used herbs that are now considered toxic, or ones that are difficult to find. I found substitutes for some of these. The note "flavour" means the substitute has a similar flavour to the origin herb; the term "usage" means the substitute is used in the same way. For example, you can use spinach any way you would prepare plantain.[90] All the ingredients that I use have a source noted here.

Source abbreviations - PD - Peri Didaxeon

Modern English Name	OLD ENGLISH NAME	Source	Ingredient Used
ale	ealu	PD, l.39.23.13.	ale or vinegar
almonds	amigdales	Pseudo-Apuleius: 30-233, l. 13.1.	almonds
anise	Pimpinella anisum[91]	Hagen 1995, p. 183.	anise seed
apple	æppel or apuldre	Bald (II), l. 30.1.6.	apple
asparagus	eorðnafala	Lacnunga, l. 15.1.	asparagus
barley	bere	Bald (III), l. 14.2.1.	barley
bayberry	lauberig	PD, l. 52.35.22.	clove (flavour)
bean	bean	Ælfric, ll. 285-302.	kidney or broad bean[92]
beef	hriðer	Bald (II), l. 43.1.6.	beef
beet	bete	Lacnunga l. 17.1.	beet
bread	hlaf	Ælfric, l. 189.	bread or breadcrumbs
broth	broþ	Bald (II), l. 26.1.7.	broth or stock
butter	butere	Ælfric, ll. 285-302.	butter
cabbage	brassica; caul	Bald (II), l. 30.1.6.	cabbage[93]
cardamom	swegles æppel	Bald (II), l. 49.29.13.	cardamom[94]

Ingredients

carrot	feldmore; more	Bald (I), l. 48.2.8.	carrot
catnip	nefte	Bald (III), l. 13.1.1.	mint (same family and flavour)
celery	merce	Lacnunga, l. 15.1.	celery
cheese	cyse	Ælfric, ll. 285-302.	cottage cheese, cream cheese, mild cheddar cheese or feta[95]
chicken	cicen; henne	PD, l. 52.35.22; Bald (II), l. 16.1.4.	chicken
cider	beor	Bald (III), l. 72.2.1.	cider or cider vinegar[96]
cinnamon	rind; romanisce rind	Recipes: Cockayne, l. 4.3.	cinnamon
clary	slarige	Lacnunga, l. 15.1.	sage (usage)
clotted cream	ream	Bald (III), l. 10.1.1.	Devonshire or clotted cream[97]
clove	Caryophyllus aromaticus	Hagen 1995, p.183.	clove
coriander	celendre	Bald (III), l. 72.2.1.	coriander
cream	flete	Bald (II), l. 10.1.1.	cream or milk
cress	cerse	Bald (II), l. 4.1.1.	cress
cucumber	hwerhwettan	Recipes: Napier, l. 4.1.	cucumber
cumin	cymen	Bald (II), l. 12.1.5.	cumin
dates	fingerappla	Hagen 1995, p. 52.	dates
dill	dile	Bald (II), l. 8.1.8.	dill
egg	æg	Ælfric, ll. 285-302.	egg
elecampane	eolene or sperewyrt	Recipes: Napier, l. 4.1.	anise (flavour)
flax seed	linsæd	Hagen 1995, p. 181.	flax seed

Ingredients

flour	smedma	Bald (I), l.31.7.1.	flour
garlic	garleac	Lacnunga l. 89.1.	garlic
ginger	gingifre	Lacnunga, l. 30.1.	ginger
gourd	cyrfæt	PD, l. 62.43.11.	cucumber (same family)
grape	winberig	Bald (II), l. 37.1.1.	raisin[98]
ham	eofor; swin	Bald (II), l. 4.1.1; Bald (II), l. 30.1.6.	pork or ham
hazel	hæsel	Lacnunga, l. 15.1.	hazelnut
honey	hunig	Bald (III), l. 9.1.2.	honey
lamb	sceap	Bald (III), l. 72.2.1.	lamb
lard	fæt	Hagen 1995, p. 76.	lard or other shortening
leek	leac; por	Bald (I), l. 39.5.6; Bald (II), l. 56.4.7.	leek
lesser celedine	wenwyrt	Bald (II), l. 4.1.1	cress (usage)
lettuce	lactuca; leahtric	Bald (I), l. 58.2.1	lettuce
malt ale	mealtealoþ	Recipes: Napier, l.4.1.	malt vinegar
marjoram	organe	Lacnunga, l. 15.1.	marjoram
mastic	hwit cudu	PD, l. 52.35.22.	cinnamon (flavour)
meal	melu	Bald (III), l. 14.2.1.	flour or meal
milk	meolce	Bald (III), l. 22.1.3.	(cow's) milk or cream
mint	mint	Bald (II), l. 12.1.5.	mint
mulberry	morberie	Medicina, l. 2.1.	mulberry[99]
mushroom	swamm	PD, l. 18.13.10.	mushroom
mustard	senep	Bald (I), l. 16.4.	mustard
oat	æt	Bald (I), l. 35.2.10.	oat

Ingredients

oil	ele	PD, l. 39.23.13.	olive or general purpose vegetable oil[100]
onion	cipe; cropleac	Bald (I), l. 39.5.6; Bald (III), l. 41.1.11.	onion
orache	melde	Lacnunga, l. 15.1.	spinach (usage)[101]
parsley	petersilian	Bald (II), l. 22.1.11.	parsley
pea	pyse	Bald (II), l. 16.1.4.	pea
pear	peru	Bald (II), l. 1.1.17.	pear
peach	persuc	Bald (II), l. 1.1.17.	peach
pennyroyal	dweorgedwostle	Lacnunga l. 17.1.	mint (same family and flavour)
pepper	pipor	Recipes: Cockayne, l. 4.3.	pepper
periwinkle	winewincle	Bald (II), l. 49.1.5.	clam (same phylum)[102]
plantain	wegbræde	Bald (II), l. 56.4.7.	spinach (usage)
poppy	popig	Bald (I), l. 82.1.1.	poppy
pork	(see ham)		
radish	ontre; rædic	Bald (I), l. 48.2.8; Lacnunga, l. 89.1.	radish
raspberry	hindberge	Bald (II), l. 51.2.2.	raspberry
rose water	rose wæter	Bald (II), l. 56.4.10.	rose water or almond extract (family)
rosehips	rosen sæd	Hagen 1992, p. 109.	rosehips or black tea[103]
rosemary	feldmædere	Latin-Old English Glossary, l. 8.147.	rosemary

rue	rude	Bald (II), l. 8.1.8.	rosemary (flavour)
rye	rige	Bald (I), l. 4.6.13.	rye
saffron	croh	Bald (II), l.37.1.1.	saffron
sage	saluian	PD, l. 63.45.30.	sage
salmon	leax	Bald (III), l. 2.3.1.	salmon
salt	sealt	Bald (I), l. 58.2.1.	salt
sausage	mearh	Bald (II), l. 30.2.3.	sausage
seed	sæd	Bald (II), l. 22.1.11.	seed
sorrel	sure	Bald (I), l. 58.2.1.	parsley (usage)
strawberry	streawberig	Bald (I), l. 2.21.16.	strawberry
sugar	triaca[104]	Hagen 1995, p. 183.	sugar
sweet-flag	marubian	Bald (III), l. 9.1.2.	cinnamon (flavour)
tansy	helde	Lacnunga, l. 15.1.	pepper (flavour)
trout	sceot	Ælfric l. 101.	trout
turnip	næp; tunnæp	Recipes: Napier, l. 4.1; Lacnunga, l. 89.1.	turnip
vinegar	eced	Bald (I), l. 16.4.	vinegar
walnut	frencissen hnutu	PD, l. 53.35.27.	walnut
water	wæter	Bald (I), l. 16.4.	water
wheat	hwæt	Bald (III), l. 22.1.3.	wheat
wild thyme	wudu cunellan	Bald (III), l. 22.1.3.	thyme (same family and flavour)
wine	win	PD, l. 62.43.11.	wine or wine vinegar
yeast	beorma	Hagen 1992, p. 15.	yeast

Bibliography

Anthimus. *De obseruatione ciborum (On the Observance of Food)*. Translated and edited by Mark Grant. Totnes, Devonshire: Prospect Books, 1996.

Ælfric, *Colloquy*. Edited by Garmonsway. N.p.: N.p., 1939, pp.18-49. Reprinted in *The Old English Corpus*. Electronic version prepared by the Dictionary of English Project. Toronto: University of Toronto, n.d.

Bald's Leechbook. Edited by Cockayne. N.p.: N.p., 1864 to 6, Vol. II, pp. 18-156 (Bk I). Reprinted in *The Old English Corpus*. Electronic version prepared by the Dictionary of English Project. Toronto: University of Toronto, n.d.

Bald's Leechbook. Edited by Cockayne. N.p.: N.p., 1864 to 6, Vol. II, pp. 174-298 (Bk II). Reprinted in *The Old English Corpus*. Electronic version prepared by the Dictionary of English Project. Toronto: University of Toronto, n.d.

Bald's Leechbook. Edited by Cockayne. N.p.: N.p., 1864 to 6, Vol. II, pp. 304-58 (Bk III). Reprinted in *The Old English Corpus*. Electronic version prepared by the Dictionary of English Project. Toronto: University of Toronto, n.d.

Better Homes and Gardens' New Cook Book. N.p.: Better Homes and Gardens Books, 1976.

Betty Crocker's Cookbook. Revised edition. Racine, WI: Golden Press, 1986.

Black, Maggie. *Food and Cooking in Medieval Britain: History and Recipes*. Birmingham: CBE Design and Print for the Historic Buildings and Monuments Commission for England, 1985.

Bristow, Pamela, ed. *The Illustrated Book of Wild Flowers*. London: Octopus Books, 1986.

Cameron, M. L. *Anglo-Saxon Medicine*. Cambridge Studies in Anglo-Saxon England, vol. 7. Cambridge: Cambridge University Press, 1993.

Bibliography

Edwards, John. *The Roman Cookery of Apicius*. Point Roberts, WA: Hartley and Marks, 1984.

Hagen, Ann. *A Handbook of Anglo-Saxon Food: Processing and Consumption*. Pinner, Middlesex: Anglo-Saxon Books, 1992.

Hagen, Ann. *A Second Handbook of Anglo-Saxon Food and Drink: Production and Distribution*. Hockwold-cum-Wilton, Norfolk: Anglo-Saxon Books, 1995.

Hall, J. R. Clark. *A Concise Anglo-Saxon Dictionary*. 4th ed. Cambridge: Cambridge University Press, 1960. Reprinted with a Supplement by Herbert D. Meritt. Toronto: University of Toronto Press for the Medieval Academy of America, 1984.

Kowalchik, Claire and Hylton, William H., ed. *Rodale's Illustrated Encyclopedia of Herbs*. Emmaus, PA: Rodale Press, 1987.

Lacnunga. Edited by Grattan and Singer. N.p.: N.p., 1952, pp. 96-130, 146-204. Reprinted in *The Old English Corpus*. Electronic version prepared by the Dictionary of English Project. Toronto: University of Toronto, n.d.

Latin-Old English Glossaries. Edited by Wright and Wülcker. 1884, no. 9. Corrections by Logeman. N.p.: N.p., 1890, pp. 316-18. Reprinted in *The Old English Corpus*. Electronic version prepared by the Dictionary of English Project. Toronto: University of Toronto, n.d.

Lust, John. *The Herb Book*. New York: Bantam Books, 1974.

Medicina de quadrupedibus. Edited by de Vriend. N.p.: N.p., 1984, pp. 234-73. Reprinted in *The Old English Corpus*. Electronic version prepared by the Dictionary of English Project. Toronto: University of Toronto, n.d.

Monthey, Marcia. "Cheeses: A History," *Tournaments Illuminated*, no. 91, pp. 31-36.

Peri Didaxeon. Edited by Löweneck. N.p.: N.p., 1896, pp. 3-53. Corrected by Sanborn 1983. Reprinted in *The Old English Corpus*. Electronic version prepared by the Dictionary of English Project. Toronto: University of Toronto, n.d.

Pseudo-Apuleius. *Herbarium*. Edited by de Vriend. N.p.: N.p., 1984, pp. 30-233. Reprinted in *The Old English Corpus*. Electronic version prepared by the Dictionary of English Project. Toronto: University of Toronto, n.d.

Bibliography

Recipes. Edited by Cockayne. N.p.: N.p., 1864 to 6, Vol. I, pp. 374-8. Reprinted in *The Old English Corpus*. Electronic version prepared by the Dictionary of English Project. Toronto: University of Toronto, n.d.

Recipes. Edited by Napier. N.p.: N.p., 1890, pp. 325-6. Reprinted in *The Old English Corpus*. Electronic version prepared by the Dictionary of English Project. Toronto: University of Toronto, n.d.

Rombauer, Irma S. and Becker, Marion Rombauer. *Joy of Cooking*. Indianapolis: Bobbs-Merrill Co., 1975.

Sass, Lorna J. *To the King's Taste*. New York: St. Martin's, 1975.

Simpson, D. P. *Cassell's New Compact Latin Dictionary*. New York: Dell Publishing, 1963.

Taylor, Norman. *Taylor's Encyclopedia of Gardening*. Boston: The American Garden Guild and Houghton Mifflin, 1956.

Whitelock, Dorothy. *English Historical Documents, Vol. I: c.500-1042*. New York: Routledge, 1979.

Notes

---

[1] Hagen 1992, pp. 53-4.

[2] Hagen 1992, p. 53. In Anglo-Saxon times, a thane was a lesser noble who held land in return for service to the king.

[3] Black, p.18

[4] Whitelock, pp. 567-8 and 581.

[5] (*Wyrta & æigra, fisc & cyse, buteran & beana & ealle clæne þingc.*) Ælfric, ll. 285-302. All translations are mine unless otherwise noted.

[6] ibid., ll. 71, and 103-106.

[7] (*. . . seoþan þa þingc þe to seoþenne synd, & brædan þa þingc þe to brædene synd.*) ibid., l. 194.

[8] (*Soþlice butan cræfte minon ælc beod æmtig byþ gesewen, & buton hlafe ælc mete to wlættan byþ gehwyred.*) Ælfric, l. 189. Ælfric wrote his *Colloquy* c. 1000.

[9] Anthimus, p. 51.

[10] "Take fayre Flowre and the whyte of Eyroun and the yolke, a lytel. than take Warme Berme, and putte al thes to-gederys and bete hem to-gederys with thin hond tyl it be schort and thikke y-now, and caste Sugre y-now ther-to, and thenne lat reste a whyle." Sass, p. 112.

[11] Hagen 1992, p. 20.

[12] Hagen 1992, pp. 20-21 and Sass, p. 17.

[13] All cup measurements given are US cups in which 8 ounces equal one cup.

[14] Hagen 1992, p. 71.

[15] *Bald* (Bk II), l. 56.4.10.

[16] *Pseudo-Apuleius*: 30-233, l. 13.1 and Andre Boorde, *Dyetary*, Ed. F. J. Furnivall, Early English Text Society, es. 10, London, 1870 as quoted in Sass, p. 128.

17 *Bald* (Bk III), l. 9.1.2.

18 *Lacnunga*, l. 30.1.

19 Hagen 1992, p.63.

20 *Bald* (Bk II), l. 12.1.5.

21 Edwards, pp.12-13.

22 For example, in *Bald* (Bk II), l. 26.1.7.

23 *Peri Didaxeon*, l. 39.23.13.

24 If you prefer to cook without alcohol, you can substitute an additional ¼ cup beef stock for the ale.

25 *Recipes*: Napier, l. 4.1.

26 Anthimus, p. 71.

27 *Bald* (Bk III), l. 14.2.1.

28 Cress is listed with other types of "easily digested food" (*eaðmelte mettas*) in *Bald* (Bk II), l. 4.1.1.

29 (*ætgædre mid geonge swines flæsce*) *Bald* (Bk II), l. 30.1.6.

30 Edwards, p. 53.

31 *Bald* (Bk II), l. 8.1.8.

32 (*Þa wyrt petersilian . . . & merces sæd . . . mid hunige sele þu him ælce dæge drincan, gif him fefer ne sie yc þæt mid wine.*) *Bald* (Bk II), l. 22.1.11.

33 *Bald* (Bk I), l. 1.16.4

34 Hagen, 1992, p.63.

35 Edwards, p.53.

36 *Bald* (Bk I), l. 58.2.1.

37 Anthimus, pp. 105-6.

38 (*. . . caules seaw, hwilum pysena broþ & eced & por mid wegbrædan gesoden & ealdne cyse gesodenne on gate meolce.*) *Bald* (Bk II), l. 56.4.7. Goat's cheese is given as a cure for headaches in *Medicina*, l. 7.6.

39 Edwards, p.61.

40 (*grene cyrfætan*) *Peri Didaxeon* l. 62.43.11.

[41] Edwards, p.62.

[42] (. . . *ecede & swiðe fæste gesoden ægra . . . & wyrta & lactucas . . . & hænne flæsc næs swiþe gesoden & . . . pysena cyn & mylsce æppla.*) *Bald* (Bk II), l. 16.1.4.

[43] Anthimus, p. 69.

[44] ibid.

[45] *Lacnunga* l. 17.1.

[46] *Lacnunga* l. 89.1.

[47] *Lacnunga* l. 60.1.

[48] *Peri Didaxeon* l. 18.13.10.

[49] *Bald* (Bk II), l. 23.1.9.

[50] Edwards, p.87.

[51] I have chosen to use salmon rather than oysters because of personal taste.

[52] Ælfric, l. 106 and *Bald* (Bk III), l. 2.3.1.

[53] Edwards, pp. 68-71.

[54] Ælfric, l. 101.

[55] *Bald* (Bk III), l. 22.1.3.

[56] Hagen 1992, p. 58 and Hagen 1995, p. 357.

[57] Anthimus, p. 69.

[58] *Peri Didaxeon*, l. 52.35.22.

[59] Clove and cinnamon were two of the spices left in Bede's will. Hagen 1995, p. 183.

[60] Hagen 1995, p. 115 and Anthimus, p. 53.

[61] Hagen 1992, pp. 41 and 55.

[62] *Bald* (Bk II), l. 4.1.1.

[63] Anthimus, p. 53.

[64] *Bald* (Bk III), l. 72.2.1.

[65] Hagen 1995, pp. 205-7.

[66] Edwards, p. 67.

[67] (*litles [cicles]*) *Peri Didaxeon*, l. 21.15.3.

[68] Edwards, p.301.

[69] Hagen 1992, p.58 and *Bald* (Bk II), l. 10.1.1.

[70] Edwards, pp. 86-93.

[71] *Lacnunga*, l. 15.1.

[72] *Peri Didaxeon*, l. 63.45.30.

[73] Edwards, p. 69.

[74] Hagen 1992, p. 62.

[75] Hagen 1992, p. 64.

[76] *Bald* (Bk II), l. 37.1.1.

[77] Anthimus, p. 51-3.

[78] Hagen 1995, pp. 192-3.

[79] Edwards, p. 83 and Sass, p. 108-9.

[80] Cockayne Recipes 1.4.3.

[81] Hagen 1992, p.63.

[82] Edwards, p. 175 and Hagen 1992, p. 62.

[83] *Bald* (Bk I), l. 59.1.8.

[84] Hagen 1992, p.20.

[85] *Lacnunga*, l. 30.1.

[86] *Bald* (Bk I), l. 2.21.16 and *Bald* (Bk II), l. 51.2.2.

[87] Hagen 1995, pp. 228 and 234.

[88] Sass, p. 28.

[89] *Bald* (Bk II), l. 8.1.8.

[90] Substitutes are based on suggestions from Kowalchik and Hylton and from Edwards.

[91] I have included the botanical names for the two spices for which I could not find the Old English names. These are anise and cloves.

[92] These are the two beans known to be used in Europe during Anglo-Saxon times. Hagen 1995, p. 37.

[93] *Brassica oleracea* was a bluish grey plant that is no longer cultivated. It was the ancestor of the modern cabbage, kale, cauliflower, broccoli and brussel sprouts.

[94] As suggested by Hagen 1995, p. 54.

[95] Cottage cheese and cream cheese are similar to that which the Anglo-Saxons called *niwe cyse* (new cheese). Some types of hard cheese date back to Roman times. One type, the Cheshire, is recorded in the *Domesday Book*. Mild (white) Cheddar has a similar mild, nutty taste and is easy to find. Goat's cheese is given as a cure for headaches in *Medicina*, l. 7.6. The Anglo-Saxons may also have eaten a cheese similar to Jarlsberg.

[96] As suggested in Hagen 1995, pp. 205-7.

[97] Hagen describes *ream* as a type of cream that was heated to thicken and preserve it. This also describes clotted cream. Hagen 1992, p. 27.

[98] Bede made a bequest of raisins. Hagen 1995, p. 53.

[99] This source actually refers separately to the tree and its fruit. "Come to the tree that one calls the mulberry tree and pick off its fruit." (*Cyme to þam treowe þe man hateþ morbeam, & of ðam nim æppel.*) The term *morberie* can be found in Hall.

[100] Olive oil was imported from the Mediterranean. Hagen 1995, p. 180.

[101] Hagen 1995, p. 41 refers to *atriplex hortensis* as spinach. This is garden orache and not the plant known by Americans as spinach (*spinacea oleracea*).

[102] I could not find reference to clams themselves. Ælfric, however, refers to another bivalve mollusk, the mussel (*muscle*) in line 106 of his *Colloquy*. This appears to be the marine bivalve and not the fresh water clam.

[103] If you are unable to find rosehips, you can use tea for the added acid in the wine. You could also use a commercial acid.

[104] This is a Late Latin term. Sugar was one of the spices listed in Bede's will.

Some of our other titles

Looking for the Lost Gods of England
Kathleen Herbert

Kathleen Herbert sifts through the royal genealogies, charms, verse and other sources to find clues to the names and attributes of the Gods and Goddesses of the early English. The earliest account of English heathen practices reveals that they worshipped the Earth Mother and called her Nerthus. The tales, beliefs and traditions of that time are still with us and able to stir our minds and imaginations.

£4-95   ISBN 1–898281–04–1   A5   64 pages

A Handbook of Anglo-Saxon Food: Processing and Consumption
Ann Hagen

For the first time information from various sources has been brought together in order to build up a picture of how food was grown, conserved, prepared and eaten during the period from the beginning of the 5th century to the 11th century. No specialist knowledge of the Anglo-Saxon period or language is needed, and many people will find it fascinating for the views it gives of an important aspect of Anglo-Saxon life and culture. In addition to Anglo-Saxon England the Celtic west of Britain is also covered. Subject headings include: drying, milling and bread making; dairying; butchery; preservation and storage; methods of cooking; meals and mealtimes; fasting; feasting; food shortages and deficiency diseases.

£9-95   ISBN 0–9516209–8–3   A5   192 pages

A Second Handbook of Anglo-Saxon Food & Drink
Production & Distribution
Ann Hagen

This second handbook complements the first and brings together a vast amount of information. Subject headings include: cereal crops; vegetables, herbs and fungi; fruit and nuts; cattle; sheep; goats; pigs; poultry and eggs; wild animals and birds; honey; fish and molluscs; imported food; tabooed food; provision of a water supply; fermented drinks; hospitality and charity. 27-page index.

Food production for home consumption was the basis of economic activity throughout the Anglo-Saxon period and ensuring access to an adequate food supply was a constant preoccupation. Used as payment and a medium of trade, food was the basis of the Anglo-Saxons' system of finance and administration.

£14-95   ISBN 1–898281–12–2   A5   432 pages

Anglo-Saxon Riddles
Translated by John Porter

This is a book full of ingenious characters who speak their names in riddles. Here you will meet a one-eyed garlic seller, a bookworm, an iceberg, an oyster, the sun and moon and a host of others from the everyday life and imagination of the Anglo-Saxons.

John Porter's sparkling translations retain all the vigour and subtly of the original Old English poems, transporting us back over a thousand years to the roots of our language and literature. This edition contains all 95 riddles of the Exeter Book.

£4-95   ISBN 1–898281–13–0   A5   112 pages

An Introduction to the Old English Language and its Literature
Stephen Pollington

The purpose of this general introduction to Old English is not to deal with the teaching of Old English but to dispel some misconceptions about the language and to give an outline of its structure and its literature. Some basic knowledge about the origins of the English language and its early literature is essential to an understanding of the early period of English history and the present form of the language. This revised and expanded edition provides a useful guide for those contemplating embarking on a linguistic journey.

£4-95   A5   ISBN 1-898281-06-8   64 pages

First Steps in Old English: An easy to follow language course for the beginner
Stephen Pollington

A complete, well presented and easy to use Old English language course that contains all the exercises and texts needed to learn Old English. This course has been designed to be of help to a wide range of students, from those who are teaching themselves at home, to undergraduates who are learning Old English as part of their English degree course. The author is aware that some individuals have little aptitude for learning languages and that many have difficulty with grammar. To help overcome these problems he has adopted a step by step approach that enables students of differing abilities to advance at their own pace. The course includes many exercises designed to aid the learning process. A correspondence course is also available.

£19   ISBN 1-898281-19-X   9½" x 6¾"/245 x 170mm   224 pages

Ærgeweorc: Old English Verse and Prose read by Stephen Pollington

This audiotape cassette can be used in conjunction with *First Steps in Old English* or just listened to for the sheer pleasure of hearing Old English spoken well.
Tracks: 1. Deor. 2. Beowulf – The Funeral of Scyld Scefing. 3. Engla Tocyme (The Arrival of the English). 4. Ines Domas. Two Extracts from the Laws of King Ine. 5. Deniga Hergung (The Danes' Harrying) Anglo-Saxon Chronicle Entry AD997. 6. Durham 7. The Ordeal (Be ðon ðe ordales weddigaþ) 8. Wið Dweorh (Against a Dwarf) 9. Wið Wennum (Against Wens) 10. Wið Wæterælfadle (Against Waterelf Sickness) 11. The Nine Herbs Charm 12. Læcedomas (Leechdoms) 13. Beowulf's Greeting 14. The Battle of Brunanburh 15. Blacmon – by Adrian Pilgrim.

£7-50   ISBN 1-898281-20-3   C40 audiotape   Old English transcript supplied with tape.

Wordcraft: Concise English/Old English Dictionary and Thesaurus
Stephen Pollington

Wordcraft provides Old English equivalents to the commoner modern words in both dictionary and thesaurus formats. Previously the lack of an accessible guide to vocabulary deterred many would-be students of Old English. *Wordcraft* combines the core of indispensable words relating to everyday life with a selection of terms connected with society, culture, technology, religion, perception, emotion and expression to encompass all aspects of Anglo-Saxon experience. The Thesaurus presents vocabulary relevant to a wide range of individual topics in alphabetical lists, thus making it easily accessible to those with specific areas of interest. Each thematic listing is encoded for cross-reference from the Dictionary. The two sections will be of invaluable assistance to students of the language, as well as those with either a general or a specific interest in the Anglo-Saxon period.

£11-95   ISBN 1-898281-02-5   A5   256 pages

Leechcraft: Early English Charms, Plantlore and Healing
Stephen Pollington

An unequalled examination of every aspect of early English healing, including the use of plants, amulets, charms, and prayer. Other topics covered include Anglo-Saxon witchcraft; tree-lore; gods, elves and dwarves.

The author has brought together a wide range of evidence for the English healing tradition, and presented it in a clear and readable manner. The extensive 2,000-entry index makes it possible for the reader to quickly find specific information.

The three key Old English texts are reproduced in full, accompanied by new translations. *Bald's Third Leechbook*; *Lacnunga*; *Old English Herbarium*.

£35 ISBN 1-898281-23-8 10" x 6¾" (254 x 170mm) hardcover 28 illustrations 544 pages

A Guide to Late Anglo-Saxon England: From Alfred to Eadgar II 871–1074
Donald Henson

This guide has been prepared with the aim of providing the general readers with both an overview of the period and a wealth of background information. Facts and figures are presented in a way that makes this a useful reference handbook.

Contents include: The Origins of England; Physical Geography; Human Geography; English Society; Government and Politics; The Church; Language and Literature; Personal Names; Effects of the Norman Conquest. All of the kings from Alfred to Eadgar II are dealt with separately and there is a chronicle of events for each of their reigns. There are also maps, family trees and extensive appendices.

£12-95 ISBN 1-898281-21-1 9½" x 6¾"/245 x 170mm, 6 maps & 3 family trees 208 pages

The English Elite in 1066 - Gone but not forgotten
Donald Henson

The people listed in this book formed the topmost section of the ruling elite in 1066. It includes all those who held office between the death of Eadward III (January 1066) and the abdication of Eadgar II (December 1066). There are 455 individuals in the main entries and these have been divided according to their office or position.

The following information is listed where available:

- What is known of their life;
- Their landed wealth;
- The early sources in which information about the individual can be found
- Modern references that give details about his or her life.

In addition to the biographical details, there is a wealth of background information about English society and government. A series of appendices provide detailed information about particular topics or groups of people.

£16-95 ISBN 1-898281-26-2 250 x 175mm / 10 x 7 inches paperback 272 pages

Rune Cards
Tony Linsell and Brian Partridge

"This boxed set of 30 cards contains some of the most beautiful and descriptive black and white line drawings that I have ever seen on this subject." *Pagan News*

"I feel sure that these Rune Cards will quickly gain the recognition and popularity they richly deserve. Here, one feels, is a package that provides everything one needs to learn how to read the runes, devised by an expert who obviously knows his subject thoroughly and whose enthusiasm successfully inspired a talented artist to transcribe the message of the rune into evocative images." *Prediction Magazine*

30 drawings by Brian Partridge
96 page booklet by Tony Linsell
£9-95   ISBN 1-898281-34-3

Peace-Weavers and Shield-Maidens: Women in Early English Society
Kathleen Herbert

The recorded history of the English people did not start in 1066 as popularly believed but one thousand years earlier. The Roman historian Cornelius Tacitus noted in *Germania*, published in the year 98, that the English (Latin *Anglii*), who lived in the southern part of the Jutland peninsula, were members of an alliance of Goddess-worshippers. The author has taken that as an appropriate opening to an account of the earliest Englishwomen, the part they played in the making of England, what they did in peace and war, the impressions they left in Britain and on the continent, how they were recorded in the chronicles, how they come alive in heroic verse and jokes.
£4-95   ISBN 1-898281-11-4   A5   64 pages

Dark Age Naval Power
A Reassessment of Frankish and Anglo-Saxon Seafaring Activity
John Haywood

In the first edition of this work, published in 1991, John Haywood argued that the capabilities of the pre-Viking Germanic seafarers had been greatly underestimated. Since that time, his reassessment of Frankish and Anglo-Saxon shipbuilding and seafaring has been widely praised and accepted.

'The book remains a historical study of the first order. It is required reading for our seminar on medieval seafaring at Texas A & M University and is essential reading for anyone interested in the subject.' F. H. Van Doorninck, *The American Neptune* (1994)

'The author has done a fine job, and his clear and strongly put theories will hopefully further the discussion of this important part of European history.'
Arne Emil Christensen, *The International Journal of Nautical Archaeology* (1992)

In this second edition, some sections of the book have been revised and updated to include information gained from excavations and sea trials with sailing replicas of early ships. The new evidence supports the author's argument that early Germanic shipbuilding and seafaring skills were far more advanced than previously thought. It also supports the view that Viking ships and seaborne activities were not as revolutionary as is commonly believed.5 maps & 18 illustrations
£14-95   ISBN 1-898281-22-X   approx. 10" x 6½" – 245 x 170 mm 224 pp

Ordering

Payment may be made by Visa, or Mastercard. Telephone orders accepted.
Payment may also be made by a cheque drawn on a UK bank in sterling.
If you are paying by cheque please make it payable to Anglo-Saxon Books and enclose it with your order. When ordering by post please write clearly.
UK deliveries add 10% up to a maximum of £2· 50
Europe – including **Republic of Ireland** - add 10% plus £1 – all orders sent airmail
North America add 10% surface delivery, 30% airmail
Elsewhere add 10% surface delivery, 40% airmail
Overseas surface delivery 6–8 weeks; airmail 5–10 days
For details of other titles and our North American distributor see our website or contact us at:

Anglo-Saxon Books

Frithgarth, Thetford Forest Park, Hockwold-cum-Wilton, Norfolk IP26 4NQ England
Tel: +44 (0)1842 828430 Fax: +44 (0)1842 828332
web site www.asbooks.co.uk   e-mail: sales@asbooks.co.uk

Þa Engliscan Gesiðas

Þa Engliscan Gesiðas (The English Companions) is a historical and cultural society exclusively devoted to Anglo-Saxon history. Its aims are to bridge the gap between scholars and non-experts, and to bring together all those with an interest in the Anglo-Saxon period, its language, culture and traditions, so as to promote a wider interest in, and knowledge of all things Anglo-Saxon. The Fellowship publishes a journal, *Wiðowinde,* which helps members to keep in touch with current thinking on topics from art and archaeology to heathenism and Early English Christianity. The Fellowship enables like-minded people to keep in contact by publicising conferences, courses and meetings that might be of interest to its members.
For further details see www.kami.demon.co.uk/gesithas/ or write to: The Membership Secretary, Þa Engliscan Gesiðas, BM Box 4336, London, WC1N 3XX England.

Regia Anglorum

Regia Anglorum is a society that was founded to accurately re-create the life of the British people as it was around the time of the Norman Conquest. Our work has a strong educational slant and we consider authenticity to be of prime importance. We prefer, where possible, to work from archaeological materials and are extremely cautious regarding such things as the interpretation of styles depicted in manuscripts. Approximately twenty-five per cent of our membership, of over 500 people, are archaeologists or historians.
The Society has a large working Living History Exhibit, teaching and exhibiting more than twenty crafts in an authentic environment. We own a forty-foot wooden ship replica of a type that would have been a common sight in Northern European waters around the turn of the first millennium AD. Battle re-enactment is another aspect of our activities, often involving 200 or more warriors.
For further information see www.regia.org or contact: K. J. Siddorn, 9 Durleigh Close, Headley Park, Bristol BS13 7NQ, England, e-mail: kim_siddorn@compuserve.com

Bede's World at Jarrow

Bede's world tells the remarkable story of the life and times of the Venerable Bede, 673–735 AD. Visitors can explore the origins of early medieval Northumbria and Bede's life and achievements through his own writings and the excavations of the monasteries at Jarrow and other sites.
Location – 10 miles from Newcastle upon Tyne, off the A19 near the southern entrance to the River Tyne tunnel. Bus services 526 & 527

Bede's World, Church Bank, Jarrow, Tyne and Wear, NE32 3DY
Tel: 0191 489 2106; Fax: 0191 428 2361; website: www.bedesworld.co.uk

Sutton Hoo near Woodbridge, Suffolk

Sutton Hoo is a group of low burial mounds overlooking the River Deben in south-east Suffolk. Excavations in 1939 brought to light the richest burial ever discovered in Britain – an Anglo-Saxon ship containing a magnificent treasure which has become one of the principal attractions of the British Museum. The mound from which the treasure was dug is thought to be the grave of Rædwald, an early English king who died in 624/5 AD.
This National Trust site has an excellent visitor centre, which includes a reconstruction of the burial chamber and its grave goods. Some original objects as well as replicas of the treasure are on display.
2 miles east of Woodbridge on B1083   Tel. 01394 389700

The Sutton Hoo Society

Our aims and objectives focus on promoting research and education relating to the Anglo Saxon Royal cemetery at Sutton Hoo, Suffolk in the UK. The Society publishes a newsletter SAXON twice a year, which keeps members up to date with society activities, carries resumes of lectures and visits, and reports progress on research and publication associated with the site. If you would like to join the Society please write to:

Membership Secretary, Sutton Hoo Society,
258 The Pastures, High Wycombe, Buckinghamshire HP13 5RS England
website: www.suttonhoo.org

West Stow Anglo-Saxon Village

An early Anglo-Saxon Settlement reconstructed on the site where it was excavated consisting of timber and thatch hall, houses and workshop. Open all year 10am–4.15pm (except Yule). Special provision for school parties. A teachers' resource pack is available. Costumed events are held at weekends, especially Easter Sunday and August Bank Holiday Monday. Craft courses are organised.
For further details see www.stedmunds.co.uk/west_stow.html or contact:
The Visitor Centre, West Stow Country Park, Icklingham Road, West Stow,
Bury St Edmunds, Suffolk IP28 6HG Tel: 01284 728718

Wuffing Education

Wuffing Education provides those interested in the history, archaeology, literature and culture of the Anglo-Saxons with the chance to meet experts and fellow enthusiasts for a whole day of in-depth seminars and discussions. Day Schools take place at the historic Tranmer House overlooking the burial mounds of Sutton Hoo in Suffolk.
For details of programme of events contact:-
Wuffing Education, 4 Hilly Fields, Woodbridge, Suffolk IP12 4DX
email education@wuffings.co.uk website www.wuffings.co.uk
Tel. 01394 383908 or 01728 688749